Terrier, Worrier

Terrier, Worrier

A Poem in Five Parts

Anna Jackson

First published 2025
Auckland University Press
Waipapa Taumata Rau
University of Auckland
Private Bag 92019
Auckland 1142
New Zealand
www.aucklanduniversitypress.co.nz

ISBN 978 1 77671 166 6

A catalogue record for this book is available from the National Library of New Zealand

Design by Greg Simpson
Illustrations by Briana Jamieson
This book was printed on FSC® certified paper
Printed in China by 1010 Printing International Ltd

Contents

Summer: Terrier, worrier 6

Autumn: Lounge scale 18

Winter: Hilbert spaces 32

Spring: Matchbox beetles 46

Summer: Memory palace 60

Notes 75

Acknowledgements 82

Summer

Terrier, worrier

I thought about the dreams I had dreamed in the night, and how I was already forgetting them but could still remember the kindness in them, and whether the kindness of the friends in the dream was really about the warmth of Simon's legs against mine.

I thought, I could get up and have breakfast. I heard the cat and I thought, hearing the cat is not a thought, it is just something I am hearing. Then I wondered whether thinking that hearing the cat wasn't a thought was itself a thought, but because I wouldn't have thought that thought if I weren't thinking about thoughts I decided it didn't count.

I had been reading *In My Mind's Eye*, Jan Morris's thought diary, in which she recorded a thought a day. When she reached 188 thoughts her thought diary ended. On day 87 she recorded that she didn't seem to have had a thought.

I heard birds and thought that although I am only hearing them, and I am not having a thought, it still feels like a thought, almost like a thought of my own, or a conversation I am having, or perhaps it is more like reading a poem, where the words, or the movement of the thought, the song of the thought, is given to you rather than coming from you, but still moves through you.

Wilma the hen was making a pet of a blackbird. She was the only hen left of our flock and I thought, I need to get more hens.

Several of Jan Morris's thought diary entries are about her Norwegian cat, Ibsen, now deceased but often remembered. 'All other cats may be just cats, but my cat Ibsen was a friend and a colleague. My cat Ibsen was different.' I thought about the strange manner in which other people's cats are just cats, and I thought, that must be what it is like for our cat Momo, who likes us but is afraid of other people, probably because other people aren't persons at all to her, but human beings, just as other cats aren't persons to me but cats.

I thought about the distinction we make between nature and culture, as if only humans have culture, but what about how differently animals learn to live when they live with people? The pet hen I had as a child joined the flock of people and cats she found in our household, working out a hybrid culture that could make sense of quite different instincts and behaviours. She maintained a place at the top of the pecking order, shooing the cats off all the beds in the morning before laying an egg in one of the warm hollows where a cat had been. The cats weren't cats to her but people, or flock members.

I told Angelina about the day Jan Morris didn't have a thought and how I wondered whether it was possible not to have a thought. Angelina said she didn't think it was possible to have a thought without writing it out. We argued about whether Jan Morris would have been recording whole thoughts she had already had before she started writing, or whether she would have been developing thoughts she might only have thought of having but wouldn't have thought out before she started writing. I wanted to argue that this would be cheating, but this was a difficult argument to win, like all arguments about cheating when there aren't any rules.

Perhaps an animal is a person who doesn't have thoughts that can be put into words, a person who only has sensations, experiences, memories, anticipations, emotions and instincts.

I decided I would only write down thoughts I had already had before I started writing. Whether including conversations counted as cheating was another question. I decided it probably was cheating, because it is almost impossible not to have thoughts in conversation.

I thought, most of the time I, too, am a person not having thoughts but only having sensations, emotions, instincts, memories and anticipations. Perhaps thoughts, being made up of language, are a form of artificial intelligence, and I am an animal infiltrated by this thought-generating technology, a person/AI hybrid.

Robert Wyatt on cheating: 'I am a real minimalist, because I don't do very much. I know some minimalists who call themselves minimalist, but they do loads of minimalism. That is cheating. I really don't do very much.'

I thought, poetry can be a form of refusal as well as openness. It can be a refusal *in* its openness, a refusal to shut down, a refusal to let thinking be limited by cultural and genre expectations. There is a poem by Muriel Rukeyser called 'Effort at Speech Between Two People', which I love for the repetition through the poem of the phrases 'I am not happy' and 'I will be open'.

When I was twenty and heartbroken my friend Diana drew me a picture of a toothbrush with teeth instead of bristles. I had completely forgotten this but it is recorded in a diary I kept at the time and surprisingly it did seem to help.

This summer, I kept dreaming about a terrier. It was not a recurring dream but a recurring terrier that appeared in dream after dream, often needing to be released from somewhere it was trapped. It did seem as if my unconscious was hard at work trying to tell me something I was repeatedly failing to grasp. I thought, a terrier is a good symbol for the work of digging up something underground but still alive.

Wilma had not been interested in me as a person when she was still part of a flock but now she looked me in the eye which is not something she had ever done when the other hens were still alive. I thought she was looking at me person to person now, whereas before she had only looked at me as an object. I thought, there is a difference between being tame, and being a friend.

There is a difference between being tame, and being a daughter.

I wondered whether I could hear 'terrier' as a version of the word 'worrier', a worrier being not someone who makes you worry but someone who themselves worries, who worries away at things like a terrier might worry away at a sock. A terrier would be someone who allows themselves actually to indulge in the feeling of terror. I tell myself, 'I am not okay, but I will be okay', but maybe I need to stop saying that and release the terror, or maybe the terrier is not myself but represents someone else's terror which needs to be heard.

I thought, it tells us something about poetry that when we need to talk to ourselves about something we don't know we know, we tell it to ourselves when we are asleep, in images we struggle to remember when we awake, and often take more than one reading to fully understand.

I brought home three young hens I named Maude, Mabel and Goldie, and put them in the small hen-house inside the larger coop, where Wilma could talk to them through the wire without threatening them, but she showed no interest in them at all, preferring to follow me back out into the garden. Maude began at once to assert herself as the dominant hen of the three little ones, issuing random reprimands to the other two.

I thought, when I watch birds all I am seeing is birds, not particular birds with personalities. I can tell the difference between a tūī and a blackbird but not between one blackbird and another, and I can't tell anything about a particular bird's personality by watching it. Yet when I think of how individual every hen is, it must be true that each blackbird has a quite distinct personality, quite unlike any other blackbird.

As the hens became more of a flock, Wilma took her place as the dominant hen in the coop, asserting herself in a way she never had before, in a way that made personality seem not innate but entirely situational. But the three little hens clearly had very different personalities even though they were brought into the coop at the same time, under the same conditions. Maude already seemed to relate to me person to person, friend to friend, looking me in the eye, talking to me, and liking to be close to my side, even though she was not yet the lead hen of the coop. Perhaps she thought Wilma was too far above her to count.

I read that birds dream about songs in their sleep, rats dream about running, and I wondered if my hens ever dreamed of me.

Autumn

Lounge scale

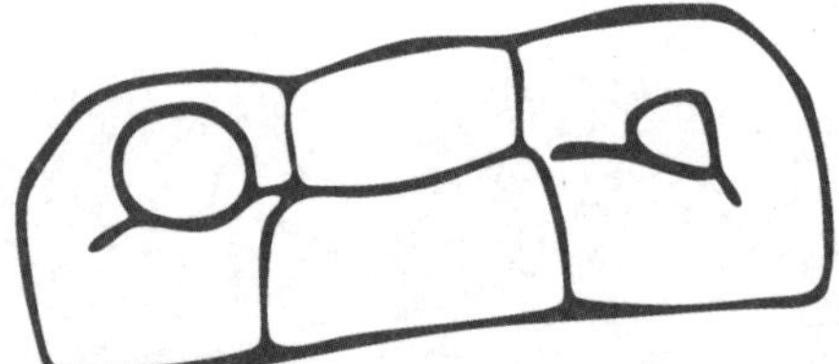

Emma told me no one her age has read a blog since 2010, everyone now listens to podcasts, and scrolls through Twitter and Instagram. We don't have the attention for blogs, she said, but I wondered if it was really an audience shift, driven by a changing capacity for attention, or whether it was the writers who are directing the shift, by choosing to present their work on different platforms? I thought, it does feel as if our attention capacity is changing, but what is changing it, if not scrolling through Twitter and Instagram?

I had a new phone with a camera and I began to take photographs of squares on my way to and from the hospital, to post on Instagram. I had not been interested in squares and now I was interested in squares and even dreamed of squares. But, I thought, interested is not the right word because there is nothing interesting about squares, there is nothing to *think* about squares.

I thought, every room is a waiting room.

I wondered if anyone wrote a diary anymore. For writers like Virginia Woolf this was a daily necessity, a form of expression so compulsive that a day without writing in the diary felt for Woolf like 'a tap left running', with it being not the writing she imagined as a running tap but the day itself, as if writing somehow stemmed the flow of time. Could the diary really have become so important to so many writers just because paper was cheap, and ready-made exercise books were sold in stationery shops? Did the diary not *answer* a need for secret self-reflection but *create* the need?

I paired my photographs of squares with quotes from what I was reading. I took a photograph of shiny red square tiles and captioned it with a quote from Madison Hamill's book *Specimen*: 'If you are afraid, you run away or play dead or stab your enemy through the heart to make the danger go away. But if you are anxious, it's because you have chosen to move in with your enemy and take up the housework of living in the danger zone.'

I thought, I feel like a kind of artist when I look out for good squares, and then find the right angle in which the squares will come out most squarely. I feel this practice orients me towards the world a little bit more like an artist than before. I wondered, are we moving towards a world in which everyone is an artist, and everyone looks for the aesthetic value in the world they inhabit and the lives they are living?

I felt like almost everyone was beginning almost everything they said with the preface, 'I feel like . . .'. I felt like they were not in fact talking about their feelings but offering opinions or thoughts, or even sometimes making plans. I wondered, what does it mean to present thoughts in terms of feelings?

I thought, how strange it was that so many scientists used to believe that animals didn't have feelings or consciousness but only followed pre-programmed instincts, when our own most powerful feelings are those we feel because of our own pre-programmed instincts – the love for our children, the fears that give children nightmares, our fears for our children's safety.

Is grief an instinct, or is it what happens when the instinct to love turns inwards, in the same way depression can be anger turned inwards towards the self?

Some feelings expand the self like a gas into the world and some condense the self into the coldest matter.

I found myself entering a conversation using the phrase 'I feel like . . .' and it felt very comfortable. Perhaps it felt comfortable because I was talking like everyone else, in the way it feels comfortable to be dressed like everyone else, but, I thought, it was also because it sounded like I wasn't presenting an argument, or making a claim that could be expected to be backed up. I was just mentioning a feeling.

But I wasn't, really. I was making a claim. I thought, it was like the way politicians talk 'around' a subject. I feel like this is a way of skirting the issue – we have conversations around a topic, rather than addressing particular points of view or points of contention.

I thought, I feel like we ought to acknowledge our feelings, but I also feel like we ought to then present thoughts, and claims, that can be challenged and which could be backed up with evidence, and we ought to act on our claims and the implications of them. And, I thought, I feel like the phrase 'I feel like' ought to introduce a simile at least as often as a thought or an opinion or a plan. I wanted to feel like a leaf but I felt like a sink full of dishes.

I photographed square concrete slabs with weeds growing in the cracks between them, pale green pistachio tiles with a pinkish tinge, one of those institutional glass door panes with a wire grid running through it, an air vent in a cream stucco wall.

I was feeling like an artist taking photos of squares for Instagram but then I read Nathan Jurgenson who wrote, 'To treat social photography solely in terms of its aesthetic quality is analogous to judging all written language on its poetic merits.' I thought, I don't even want to judge all *poetry* in terms of its poetic merits. And, I thought, social photography is less like all written language (in contrast to the subset of poetry) than it is like language in general (in contrast to the subset of only written language). It is a new form of conversation, 'a kind of visual speaking', in Jurgenson's words.

I thought, if social photography was a new form of language, does it have a grammar? One of the questions most central to animal language studies is whether animal communication ever has a grammar, or is just a series of coded sounds or gestures. What does it mean if on social media we are communicating more and more without grammar?

I thought, maybe the way to get more people to switch to solar power would be if solar panels could be another mode of communication. People pay quite a lot to keep up their data plans, so they can post images and messages on social media. What if we could light up our solar panels to print messages, in little alphabet-cells, and with colours we could adapt like octopuses to present our messages in the right emotional tone?

A psychology experiment I read about involved people moving little figures around in models of houses, instructed to imagine themselves that size and to make the figures do what they themselves would ordinarily do in that space. They were asked to keep doing this for half an hour, but they were given no clock, just told to stop when they felt they'd been going for about that long. Their sense of time turned out to be almost exactly proportionate to the scale of the model they were asked to work with: if they were working with a 1:12 model, they thought they'd been moving figures around for thirty minutes after five minutes; if a 1:24 model, it only took two and a half minutes for them to think the time must be up.

I thought about how fast time flew when I tried writing fiction, and wondered, if the speed of time was proportionate to the scale of the model, why my fictional characters were so little in my head. I had thought I was imagining them out in the world, at a 1:1 scale, picturing the fictional world being as large as the world I live in. Are the stories I make up all actually contained in a head-sized space? But isn't the real world outside me also contained in the head-sized space in which I perceive it?

I thought that I couldn't imagine my thoughts as originating anywhere in the body than the brain, even though I knew in other times people had believed thoughts originated in the gut, or that they came from the heart. I wondered what it would feel like to imagine you were thinking from the heart, would the thoughts feel less located in the head, behind the eyes?

When someone doesn't want to be photographed, it is their face they cover, even though the rest of them is still just as visible. Their hands, in front of their face, are more visible than ever.

I thought, even if the mind is a construction of activity of the brain it makes no more real sense to think of thoughts as being located in the head than it does to think of them as located in the heart. They aren't material things that can be there behind the eyes, and why behind the eyes except that I look at the world through the eyes and so I locate myself there?

When Amy told me she had dreamed about me, I felt as if my own life were like that dream in which you climb some stairs in your house and discover a whole additional room, or a whole series of rooms, you didn't know was there.

I thought maybe this could be another way of thinking about what it is like after death, a life that takes place in the dreams of other people.

I thought, this could be a new kind of biography, a biography of the dreams people have had about someone, which might tell you as much as anything else they would say about them, as much as their waking judgements of the person's character or their memory of how the person behaved at a party once.

If sometimes I think of thoughts as being behind the eyes, sometimes I think of them more as floating, in a kind of cloud around the outside of my head.

When I think of my thoughts as floating, I think of the word 'floating' too, so the idea of where my thoughts are becomes an idea that involves the sound of an o, the sound of the f and the l, the whole two syllables of the word 'floating', its balanced up-and-down rhythm, but most of all, its soft extended o sound. Thoughts *float* and then they float in language. And since we wouldn't have thoughts without language, it makes more sense to think of thoughts as residing in language than in the head.

I thought, I feel like a pillow with no head on me, a carpet with dust swept under it, a screen with words inflicting themselves on me, one dark letter at a time.

Winter

Hilbert spaces

I thought, if I can't reconcile myself to my non-existence after death by thinking about my non-existence before I was born, given that as far as time goes I am only travelling in one direction, perhaps I could reassure myself by thinking about my non-existence elsewhere in the world, in the lives I am not living in other countries, where I am not seeing the milk that spilt on the tiles or feeling that gust of wind blow by, or listening to what someone would have been leaning over, intently, to say to me, if I existed in their life.

I thought the reason I was not sleeping late was because I had nothing to dream about, going out into the world so little and having so little going on.

I thought, perhaps the rats and birds in the dream-science laboratory also woke early, electrodes on their heads, not feeling like sleeping any later even if all they had to wake up to was another day of running mazes and learning notes.

The hens were roosting earlier and earlier as the days were growing shorter, and sleeping later. I thought, if sleeping was really for the consolidation of learning, birds wouldn't sleep so much longer in winter than in summer. And, I thought, bears hibernating through the winter probably aren't processing more knowledge than they had access to when the days were longer, or managing particularly troubled or repressed emotions that they had failed to process all summer.

I thought about using the long sleeping hours of my hens to accustom them to being patted, by patting them on their perches when they were relaxed and half asleep, except they roost so high up that by the time I'd climbed up to where I could reach them they would probably be in a state of high alarm, as well as tired.

I thought, perhaps dreaming really is just like reading with your eyes shut, a way of getting through a time in which it isn't safe to move around in the world, a way of staying put.

I don't believe in an afterlife but on the question of how old I would be in it, I think it would vary the way it does in dreams, when sometimes I am a child, sometimes in my twenties or thirties, only occasionally the age I am now. In dreams I think it depends on whoever else you are dreaming about, and who you are in relation to them.

I wondered whether the hens ever dreamed of themselves at earlier ages of their lives, whether Wilma dreamed of herself under her mother's wing in the coop where she was born, whether the three younger hens ever dreamed of the incubator.

This was a time when first my mother, then my sister, then my father each took a turn at death's door.

My father said that when he was lying alone in the hospital bed wondering if he was dying, he thought of Shakespeare's Mistress Quickly recounting how Falstaff died, clutching at flowers and babbling of green fields, his nose sharp as a pen. She brought him blankets to warm his feet, which were cold as stone. She then felt to his knees, and they, too, were cold as stone. She felt her way up his body, upwards and upwards, and all she felt was cold as stone.

I read a memoir of early motherhood in which the writer consoled herself about the fact that her baby was too young to form a memory of her singing to him, by thinking that this time was forming his character and so in that way it still counted for something. This made me too angry to keep reading.

I thought, if a moment with someone only counts if it will be remembered, what about when the people we spent those moments with die and don't remember any of them anymore. Do they not count for anything?

When my daughter promised to support me through my grief, it felt like cheating, because there was no grief as terrible as not seeing my daughter.

I thought, every room is an emergency room.

I thought, people say being brave isn't about being unafraid, that you can only be brave if you are afraid, but this isn't the way we think about other qualities, like honesty, or kindness. I thought, it doesn't take anything away from someone's kindness if it is so natural to them that they would find it harder not to be kind.

When things are bewilderingly worse than makes any sense it is easy to despair, because how can you know what to do about a situation which is so much worse than any accounting can account for? But, I thought, perhaps it is bewilderingly worse than it could be because all of the factors that ought to make it less worse than it is are simply not in play. It isn't that those factors are not real, and it isn't that they mean nothing, and it isn't that you haven't accounted for other factors, besides the ones you have accounted for, that make the situation you are faced with inevitable. It is just that some of the factors that you would have thought would have counted for more in making things better aren't currently in play, but will come back into effect as other factors shift.

In other words, everything that ought to be making things better than they are *will* eventually make things better than they are. This was a hopeful thought.

I thought, people can be more or less sociable without anyone saying you are only sociable if you see people when you really don't want to. I don't complain that it isn't friendliness if you actually like hanging out with me, I don't want to only see people who are making a particular effort to see me but would much rather not.

She came upstairs looking more like a cloud than a silver lining.

Reports of near-death experiences – which could as accurately be called death experiences, since they take place after cardiac arrest, before resuscitation – seem to suggest consciousness outlives the body, but then I read about the new studies in neuroscience which found that in the last moments of life, even sometimes after days, or months, on life support with almost complete brain inactivity, there is an extraordinary final explosion of brain activity, a fireworks of synaptic firing, that lasts for minutes after the body dies.

The parts of the brain that are active when we move through the world light up at death and communicate with the parts of the brain involved in memory formation, along with the parts of the brain associated with empathy. So perhaps those near-death – or death – experiences of travelling outside the body and into white light are taking place inside the mind after all.

At the funeral of a friend's father, Sasha was telling me about their work with Hilbert spaces, the mathematical study of infinite dimensions within finite spaces.

I thought, an evolutionary purpose for the wild synaptic firings of the dying brain is hard to imagine but it is pretty much exactly the fireworks we might expect if in that near-death moment our finite consciousness really did encounter the infinite dimensions of the divine.

I thought, I can believe in God the way mathematicians believe in imaginary numbers. It isn't that I think there is anything real that God corresponds to, but the idea of God allows thoughts to be thought out to a truth that couldn't otherwise be reached.

I thought, I can understand a concept like loyalty, or nobility, or sacrifice by what it has to mean aesthetically, for a work of literature to work *as* a work of literature. It's like the way we can work out how words were pronounced from the demands of a rhyme scheme or a poem's metre. I can love the place of the concept within the aesthetic order of the text without having any allegiance to the concept outside the text. It is a suspension not of disbelief but of value.

I wondered why you can't read in your dreams, and thought, it must be for the same reason no one uses a cell phone in dreams, or can drive a car: there is something technology-shy about dreams.

I asked Simon if cars in his dreams always turn into pedal cars, the way they do in mine, but he said no, he drove cars in his dreams, just usually over a cliff.

I dreamed I was hiding under a desk in an empty school room, knowing if I were discovered I would have acid poured over me. That dream, I thought on first waking, was about Twitter, but on further thought I wondered if it was a dream about dreaming itself, if consciousness could be thought of as the desk under which we hide when we are awake.

'Thought stalls on an event it cannot bear to contemplate, can go no further', Jacqueline Rose wrote in her book *On Not Being Able to Sleep*. 'The task of psychoanalysis is not so much to undo forgetting, but to put poetry back into the mind.' She could have said the same about the task of dreaming, psychoanalysis without the analysis.

I thought, perhaps it isn't that people high on mushrooms are accessing some transcendent truth through the unlocking of their own minds, perhaps it is that they are experiencing life the way fungi experience it, with a consciousness without individual identity, dispersed and without borders.

To imagine a language, Wittgenstein wrote, is to imagine a form of life. He gives the example of a language made up of commands and reports from battle, or a language made up only of questions to which you can give a yes or no answer. I thought, the forms of life, or ways of living, he is imagining are easier to work out from these examples than the languages. What kind of grammar could restrict conversation to commands while allowing reports from battle?

I thought, wouldn't someone whose grammar allowed reports from battle have the idea of reporting on other activities? Wouldn't someone whose language was made up of questions think of using the question mode rhetorically, until someone eventually thought to reply to a 'question' with a 'question'?

Then as soon as I stopped thinking about armed nation states and a world of online bureaucracy and opened the doors to the waiting pets, in at once rushed forms of life speaking only in commands and questions.

Spring

Matchbox beetles

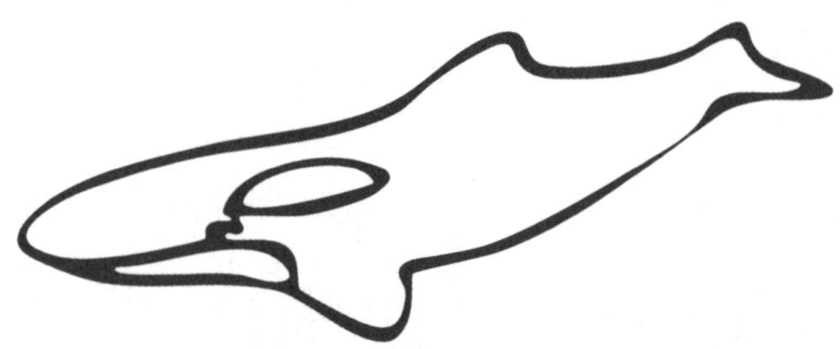

When I was arguing with Simon about why it would be better to leave doors open I felt as though this was a joke, a provocation, because obviously doors should be shut, and yet everything I said was true, and I *would* prefer all the doors to be left just slightly ajar.

I thought about how I only remember any of these thoughts because I wrote them down and how on days I don't write down thoughts I don't remember any at all, but when I do start writing down any I remember others come back to me, as if they are kept, for a while, in a kind of temporary storage.

I wondered whether noticing what they are thinking, or even noticing *that* they are thinking, is what makes adolescents so attractive and whether this is why they all fall in love with each other.

Agnes asked if meaning drains out of life as you get older, and almost everyone said no, except for me. I answered emotionally, not logically, and even as I was answering yes I was thinking, but is a novel drained of meaning in its last few chapters? Is a sonnet drained of meaning after the volta?

If life isn't drained of meaning as you get older, why do so many novels end when the characters are still young, why does a Shakespearean comedy end with the marriages of one young character to another, and all their lives ahead of them?

I thought about how listening to music feels like listening to emotion, and I wondered if the reverse is also true and every emotion has its musical equivalent? If a kind of omniscient, godlike composer were able to tune in to our every emotion, could every one of us be supplied with the musical score of our every moment?

I thought, if it were as mechanical as that there wouldn't even be a need for the godlike composer (though what a way to think of God!), it would just be a matter of coding and any computer could do it. But are we *always* feeling emotions, or do we occasionally feel emotions in bursts of song punctuating the day? Would the music-generating translation-program be a constant play of music, or long stretches of silence with longer or shorter musical interludes?

I wondered, is 'neutral' an emotion, and does it have a tune to it, that would play for much of the day? Is 'neutral' really contentment, a contentment that isn't being attended to?

I thought, it is true that a tragedy isn't drained of meaning any more than a comedy is, and regret is an emotion that has at least as much aesthetic depth as hope, but I would rather pattern my life on a Shakespearean Romance, with all losses restored, all relationships renewed, all daughters found and wives turned back from stone.

I thought, longing is the most meaningful feeling, because it looks both forwards and backwards. When you long for something, it is more than a hope for something in the future, because aren't you always longing for something you lost, that you hope to restore?

I thought, Effective Altruists measure effectiveness by how much happiness it results in, and so some come to the conclusion that the most Effective Altruism involves making sure the most lives get born, so that instead of working to reduce poverty now, they are raising money to make sure humanity will be able to escape the solar system when we need to get out, but I don't think you can add up happiness, not even in a single life.

I photographed a floor softly tiled in white and grey and posted it with a quote from Emily Brontë's diary: 'Aunt has come into the kitchen just now and said, "Where are your feet Anne?" Anne answered, "On the floor Aunt."'

I thought, we take it as axiomatic that happiness is the highest good, but for the Romans it was justice, for the Greek philosophers it was knowledge. For me, I think it is beauty.

For Hannah Arendt, beauty has a political importance because it is a truth that can be argued for. To call something beautiful is to make a judgement that can be held to the potential criticism of others, that might need to be explained, that to be persuasive draws on shared ideas and ideals. It is this sharing, criticising, arguing and persuading that makes aesthetic judgement political, because it builds community. I thought, this seems to leave out beauty.

A whale, singing, will hang vertically in the water, following one complete song with another until it needs to surface to breathe. They won't usually interrupt a song to breathe, and if they do will breathe between different themes of the song, quickly tucking a breath in between notes the way a person singing will, so as not to break the melody.

Songs are copied amongst groups of whales, changing over the course of a season, borrowed from one whale population by another. Australian whale songs are the most popular globally, though adapted by different whale cultures with additional verses and choruses.

It is supposed that the male singers sing to attract the female whales but there is a problem with this theory, which is that the female whales don't seem very interested.

Oliver Sacks tells the story of a man, struck by lightning, who, having had no special interest in music, afterwards developed a passion for piano music, first to listen to, then to play, then to compose. 'It's like a frequency, a radio band. If I open myself up, it comes. I want to say, "It comes from Heaven", as Mozart said.'

An inability to experience music as music can come on just as suddenly. One minute music is sounding like music, the next it sounds like a toneless banging, with a metallic reverberation. I thought, how strange that music sounds metallic, without the gift for hearing music coming into play.

I wondered if there were ever tone-deaf sparrows, or whales for whom the ocean resounded with nothing but a metallic banging.

I read that sparrows appear to each other not as brown birds, but as birds shimmering with blue.

I wondered if the pets spoke in commands and questions to each other, as well as to me, and if they spoke in commands and questions even in conversations with themselves? Or do they think to themselves in music, composing their emotions like my imaginary composer-God?

I thought, maybe the female whales are singing silently to themselves.

I photographed square window-panes showing no reflection at all, wire in a diamond pattern with a tight squared plastic mesh behind it, a feather caught in a grid of chicken-wire.

Could an animal have a private language? According to Wittgenstein, no one can have a private language, and to prove this point he asks us to imagine having private beetles. If everyone has a beetle in a matchbox but no one could look inside anyone else's matchbox, how could we know we were using the word 'beetle' to talk about the same thing?

For Wittgenstein, language is a series of gestures used to provoke actions in others. What action could the word 'beetle' provoke, in Wittgenstein's world of private beetles? I thought, maybe the word 'beetle' might provoke you to wonder what other secrets I am keeping, as well as a private beetle, and perhaps whether I have a private language of my own to keep my secrets in.

Wittgenstein told a story about a diarist who uses the letter S to signify a sensation there are no words for, a sensation he wanted to record the recurrences of, so he could track its frequency for himself. Wittgenstein's argument against the possibility of a private language rests on the impossibility of giving a definition for this sign S.

Is it really impossible, he asks himself? 'I speak, or write the sign down, and at the same time I concentrate my attention on the sensation – and so, as it were, point to it inwardly.' Isn't this a definition? No, he decides, it can only be a 'ceremony', since a definition 'serves to establish the meaning of a sign' and the definition of a word can only be tested by the results of speaking it. If someone brings you an apple when you expected a pear, you know you have got the word for pear wrong.

One of my earliest memories is of being asked to bring my mother a couple of apples, and not knowing how many apples there were in a couple, I brought as many apples as I could carry, more in fact than I could carry. My mother's surprise at the apples rolling on the floor was how I learnt a couple of apples was the same as a pair.

I thought, it is a funny idea that language needs to be tested to be language at all, that unless we can be sure we are testing it against whatever everyone else means we are only babbling in words that are not words, even if, unlike Wittgenstein's diarist, we might be using words we have heard, only using them wrongly. Wittgenstein's diarist's use of the sign S made me think about how much more there is to language than communication, how by using it for inward pointing we can open up the whole vast matchbox of the self.

As for those lonely beetles, never meeting another beetle, what do they make, I wondered, of our intermittent presence as we look to see whether our indescribable beetles are still in their boxes? Do they take the flashes of light as communication? Are they working on a hermeneutics of the box openings?

Summer

Memory palace

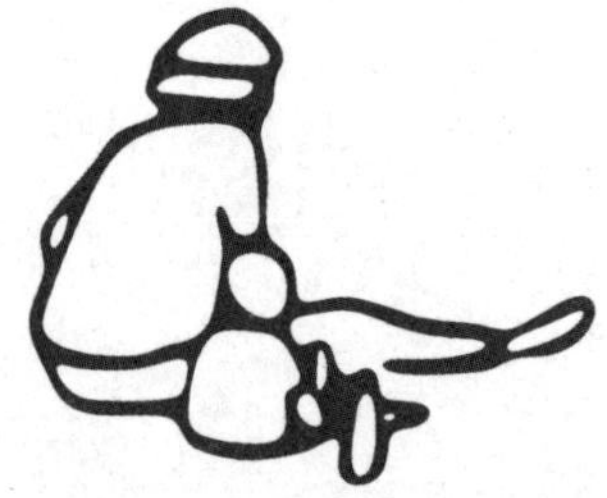

I dreamed that my mother wanted me to write to my daughter about her opinion that the train lines ought to go around the city, not through the city, and how I started writing this to my daughter even though I had been thinking myself that I wished the trains stopped more frequently at all the smaller stations in the city.

One friend said she would almost prefer not to breathe easily than feel her personality changed on steroids, another friend found the regular withdrawal from steroids the hardest part of her treatment, suffering from the same loss of energy welcomed by the other.

One friend said she was never angry and couldn't understand people getting angry with her. I thought, if anger can be turned inwards and experienced as depression, can anger turned outwards give rise to joy?

I thought about how babies have to learn the difference between their self and the rest of the world, and I thought our fantasies of magic – of being able to shift the world about you through the power of mental focus, or of making things come to you and obey you at your command – describe what it must have felt like when you first drew that hand towards your mouth, or found you could bring your mother into your presence by the power of your voice.

I thought about the concept of 'peripersonal space', the idea that your mental mapping of the self includes the immediate space around you, and what you habitually keep about your person, including for instance your bag, or your falcon.

Renaissance falconry manuals stress the importance of keeping a young falcon close to the falconer's body, with 'a continual carrying of them upon your fist', as well as 'a most familiar stroaking and playing with them, with the Wing of a dead Foule or such like'. In this way, the falcon and the falconer's bodies become merged in a single shared peripersonal space, from where, when the falcon soars after its prey, it must feel to the falconer as if they, too, have taken wing.

It was thought of songbirds that only the male birds sang. But when female scientists started looking, they found female songbirds in one species after another. It turned out that the dominance of male songbirds is only true in the northern hemisphere, where Darwin and other early ornithologists were from, and for a century, no one questioned the belief only male birds sang.

When women began listening, they found that in the northern hemisphere, too, female songbirds were singing, just more quietly and at different times to the male birds.

I remembered a bird I sang a duet with when I was a child, the two of us taking turns to sing the song I thought I had taught it. Years later, in another city, I heard it again, sung by a grey warbler.

I thought, if a falcon can be part of your peripersonal space, can birdsong be peripersonal?

I thought, can a poem be peripersonal, or a dream?

Sometimes I used to dream I was angry with my mother, and when I woke up I wondered if it meant I was repressing my anger at her in real life, but now I think my dreaming self had just picked her as the safest person my anger could be directed at.

I thought of how Virginia Woolf came to terms with her anguish over not having children by thinking the anguish itself was a physical symptom, that if she had not been childless, she would have found something else to attach the anguish to. I found it consoling to think that the shame that consumed me in the night could have been about anything, that if I had not made the mistakes I had made, the same amount of shame would have attached itself to some lesser mistake.

But not very consoling.

Beside my bed there is a painting of a blue fish, floating high above a grey-blue sea, impaled on a grey-blue spike. On the back of the painting are written the words of the artist, my daughter, aged 3: 'This is the fish. I painted it because it stuck in my mind.'

I was seeing a massage therapist for pain in the neck and shoulders but she stopped after half an hour at a point on my lower back and waited. She waited a long time and I waited too. I thought, every body is a waiting room. 'Do you feel it?' she asked.

And then it began, a coldness starting to move in me, like smoke, the slightest movement at first, an unravelling, a quickening, that became a torrent, and I was flooded with feeling, heaving with it, the tears pouring out of my eyes, the sound I was making nothing I could control, and all of this went on for almost an hour but there was nothing I could do but live it out till it was over.

I thought, every body is an emergency room.

The menopause test included the question, do you feel you are unloved? I thought, but what if I *am* unloved?

Instructions for training your falcon include 'gazing often and looking at them in the face, with a loving and gentle Countenance'.

I thought, when Mabel looks me in the eye, I always feel she is about to peck at it.

I have never regretted having either of my children, but I have regretted, once or twice, every single pet.

In the book I was reading about whales, the idea was floated that one day we might use computer programs to learn how to communicate with them. Then I saw on the news that AI had, indeed, learnt how to communicate with whales, and could successfully predict what the next move would be in a whale conversation. The only problem was, we still didn't know what they were saying, the whales or the AI program conversing with them.

I remember sitting in the back seat of the car and hearing my parents talking in the front seat and realising I was understanding what they were saying. This was a revelation – until then I had thought they needed to be talking directly to me for me to understand them.

I remember crying long after I could remember what I was crying about, determined not to give in.

I remember making a doctor's appointment when I was seventeen, because I didn't seem to be having thoughts anymore. I thought it might be a medical problem.

I remember sitting in the car after work, not wanting to turn on the windscreen wipers because I felt like I needed the rain on the windscreen to do the work of crying for me.

I thought, every body is a memory palace.

I dreamed I was in conversation with a photographer who had been photographing a series of traumatic scenes, a series of photographs both terrible and beautiful. But, before he could exhibit them, before he could even print them, he exposed all the film, and all the images were lost. Now, he wondered, did he have to go through everything again, re-enact the scenes, in order to recreate the images?

I thought, I don't know why I translate Catullus over and over again, but it happens and I feel it, I feel like I am split in two.

I thought, when I am Catullus, writing as Sappho, as Ariadne, as Attis, as Procne, am I bird or birdsong? The journey, or the backwards glance?

I sat in the car with my daughter, tears running down our faces. Then I laughed, and turned the windscreen wipers off.

When I arrived home, I found the hens were working on transforming the bank into a series of dust baths, Mabel leading the way from one to the next, Wilma keeping one dust bath behind.

A pecking order isn't as simple as a chain of dominance in which each hen maintains its position over the hen immediately below it on the chain. It is based not only on feelings of rivalry but also on feelings of friendship and antipathy, which don't always align completely neatly with their sense of relative power. I wondered if Wilma ever missed Brownie, who had been her closest friend.

Lying on the carpet in our living room, Simon cooking in the other room, I had the most profound sense of contentment. I realised I was in the position I spent much of my childhood in, lying on a carpet, able to play the most complicated imaginary games in front of everyone, with whatever props were to hand, knowing that even with the outer workings of my inner life on display I was completely private because no one was remotely interested.

The child psychologist D. W. Winnicott called this feeling of safety being 'alone in the presence of the mother', and it is this sense of being alone in the presence of the world I think I look for in writing now.

I read that the reason time exists is that heat cannot pass from a cold body to a hot body if nothing else around it changes.

Then it was morning again, and the pets were making their feelings known. Simon had been dreaming about zombies that were impossible to tell apart from humans. 'Then how did you know they were zombies?' 'Because they were chasing me.' 'Did you get away?' 'Yes. I tricked them.' 'How?' 'I told them to go that way' – pointing the other way.

Notes

Summer: Terrier, worrier

Jan Morris, *In My Mind's Eye: A Thought Diary*, Faber, 2019.

'My cat Ibsen was different', Jan Morris, *In My Mind's Eye*, p. 12.

Robert Wyatt on cheating, quoted in 'Dead moles in their holes', an article by Wesley Stace, reviewing Marcus O'Dair's biography, *Times Literary Supplement*, 12 December 2014.

Muriel Rukeyser, 'Effort at Speech Between Two People', just an astonishing poem, hard to believe it was published in 1935, it would feel innovative now, with its colons all over the show and its gaps on the page, and its extraordinary lines, written when she was 21! And look at these lines, from another poem 'The Speed of Darkness':

> Big-boned man young and of my dream
> Struggles to get the live bird out of his throat.
> I am he am I?   Dreaming?
> I am the bird am I?   I am the throat?

You can find these poems by Rukeyser, and more, on the Poetry Foundation website: poetryfoundation.org

Autumn: Lounge scale

Virginia Woolf, Sunday 15 February 1919, after not having written in her diary since 4 February: 'What a disgraceful lapse! Nothing added to my disquisition, & life allowed to waste like a tap left running. Eleven days unrecorded.' (*The Diary of Virginia Woolf, Volume One: 1915–1919*, Anne Olivier Bell (ed.), Penguin, 1979, p. 239.)

I wrote about Virginia Woolf's diary poetics in my book *Diary Poetics* (Routledge, 2009). I used to write a diary myself, in my twenties, until I started writing about diaries instead, and stopped keeping my own. Though the other thing that happened was I persuaded Simon to keep a diary, and I read his and he read mine and we very nearly broke the marriage off. The tap has been left running ever since. Eventually it will run itself dry.

Squares: I have stopped photographing squares but you can probably still see my photographs, with quotes from what I was reading, on instagram.com/poetry_was_a_grid/

Madison Hamill, *Specimen*, a very wonderful collection of essays (Victoria University Press, 2020, p. 150).

Nathan Jurgensen, *The Social Photo: On Photography and Social Media*, Verso, 2019, pp. 23, 27.

Lounge scale: I read about lounge scale in Susan Stewart's book *On Longing: Narratives of the Miniature, the Gigantic, the Souvenir, the Collection* (Duke University Press, 1992).

Winter: Hilbert spaces

The memoir was by Clover Stroud. I did pick it up again, but I read it fairly cursorily.

On bravery: I do think I have a point, but I also can see that there is a courage in facing fears that being fearless wouldn't require. (And in going to parties.)

Reports of near-death experiences: I've always planned to head towards that white light, I can tell you. This particular article on the neuroscience of near-death experiences was in *The Guardian*: 'The new science of death: "There's something happening in the brain that makes no sense"', by Alex Blasdel, 2 April 2024.

Infinite dimensions within finite spaces: you can read about them by googling Hilbert spaces, but I found out about them through Sasha.

Jacqueline Rose, *On Not Being Able to Sleep: Psychoanalysis and the Modern World*, Princeton University Press, 2003, p. 7.

Ludwig Wittgenstein, *Philosophical Investigations*, G. Anscombe (trans.), Basil Blackwell, 1958. You can find the text, in English, out of copyright, online. It is in little paragraphs, so it is very easy to read. Here's paragraph 327: '"Can one think without speaking?" – And what is *thinking*? – Well, don't you ever think? Can't you observe yourself and see what is going on? It should be quite simple. You do not have to wait for it as for an astronomical event and then perhaps make your observation in a hurry.'

Spring: Matchbox beetles

When is a door not a door? I considered 'When is a door' as a title for this book, as a statement rather than half a question, but with the idea you'd probably be picturing the door as ajar. (Or, how about 'Woman as gates' from Rukeyser's 'Käthe Kollwitz' –

> Woman as gates, saying:
> 'The process is after all like music,
> like the development of a piece of music...')

Agnes is the philosopher Agnes Callard, and the question about whether life drains of meaning as you get older was a Twitter poll she set in 2020. Was she wondering for herself? Was it to answer an argument? Though it would only answer an argument with opinions. By people like me! Or, as it turned out, mostly unlike me, at least regarding their thoughts on the draining of meaning out of life.

Agnes Callard asked in another Twitter poll, would you turn up at a protest even if you knew it wouldn't be instrumental in bringing about the change the protest was calling for? I said yes, in the same way that I would turn up to a funeral even if I didn't believe it would bring anyone back to life.

Is 'neutral' an emotion? I think it is funny I think that I don't have emotions, just as I think that I don't have thoughts. It seems I do have thoughts, so perhaps I have emotions too.

Effective Altruism: see *Strangers Drowning: Impossible Idealism, Drastic Choices, and the Urge to Help*, by Larissa MacFarquhar (Penguin, 2016).

'Aunt has come into the kitchen', Katherine Frank, *A Chainless Soul: A Life of Emily Brontë*, Houghton Mifflin, 1990, p. 86.

A whale, singing, hangs vertically: This was in the wonderful book *How to Speak Whale: A Voyage into the Future of Animal Communication*, by Tom Mustill (Grand Central Publishing, 2022), as were the facts about the popularity of Australian whale songs and the theory of whale seduction.

'It's like a frequency, a radio band' is in Oliver Sacks, *Musicophilia: Tales of Music and the Brain* (Knopf, 2007). See also Maggie Rogers on writing music: 'It's like a puzzle. If you can keep your focus on it long enough, it appears. It's *right there* – but the second your brain moves it's gone.' This was from an article on Maggie Rogers in the *New Yorker*, by Amanda Petrusich, 8 April 2024.

Toneless banging: also from *Musicophilia*. This happened to Oliver Sacks himself! Also to Nabokov.

Sparrows shimmering with blue: I'm pretty sure this also was in the Tom Mustill book!

Wittgenstein, still from the *Investigations*, remark 258.

Summer: Memory palace

Can anger, turned outwards, give rise to joy? I am thinking of all the scenes in YA fantasy where the protagonist discovers magical powers they didn't know they had, when they access a powerful rage that has been building in them and that finally finds release in a fantastic, pyrotechnical display of the impossible.

There's also a terrific scene in Olivia Laing's *Crudo* (Picador, 2018) in which the husband, nervy and cross all day after being short-listed for a prize, finally explodes in anger when he is given a parking ticket, and although it might seem reasonable to be given a parking ticket when you have in fact parked on double yellow lines, he is outraged, furious, that he should get a ticket for parking on his *own street*. This is narrated by Kathy, newly wed to him, and I think what makes it feel so celebratory is how much she seems to relish the comedy of his unreasonableness, and then she goes out in the garden to fiercely behead some dahlias.

I think that if anger is a kind of self-assertion, it makes sense he is angry to be short-listed for a prize he didn't ask for, given how this places him in the position of being judged by others rather than by his own standards, making a supplicant of him by this short-listing he hasn't sought out.

Peripersonal space and falcon training: from 'Going to the Birds: Animals as Things and Beings in Early Modernity', by Marcy Norton, in *Early Modern Things: Objects and Their Histories, 1500–1800*, Paula Findlen (ed.), Taylor & Francis, 2020, pp. 57–58.

It was thought of songbirds... This, also, was from Tom Mustill's wonderful book on whales! (He is sometimes a little digressive.)

Virginia Woolf, in her diary. I cannot find the place.

Do you feel you are unloved? (When is adore not adore?) This is a genuine medical question you get asked if you see your GP about menopause symptoms. Australasian Menopause Society questionnaire, nzgp-webdirectory.co.nz/site/nzgp-webdirectory2/files/pdfs/AMS_Diagnosing_Menopause_Symptom_score_sheet_2015.pdf

D.W. Winnicott, from 'On the Capacity to be Alone', in *The Maturational Processes and the Facilitating Environment*, Hogarth Press and the Institute of Psycho-Analysis, 1965, p. 30. And from 'Dreaming, Fantasying and Living', in *Playing and Reality* (Routledge, 1971, p. 62), this comment that he quotes a patient saying to her analyst (him): 'She said: "People use God like an analyst – someone to be there while you're playing."'

The reason time exists: bbc.com/future/article/20221003-why-does-time-go-forwards-not-backwards. Alarmingly, Carlo Rovelli is quoted in this article as remarking that time's arrow really only lasts a very little time. Eventually, 'stars will stop burning, nothing will happen anymore.'

Or, as Elisa Gabbert writes, in *The Self Unstable* (Black Ocean, 2013, p. 83), 'The future isn't anywhere, so we can never get there. We can only disappear.'

Acknowledgements

First of all I would like to thank Sam Elworthy, Lauren Donald, Sophia Broom and Katharina Bauer at AUP for their enthusiastic support for this little book from the start and for their poet-level attention to detail throughout the process. Thank you to Louise Belcher for her brilliant editing. Thank you to Greg Simpson for the beautiful book design, and thank you to Briana Jamieson for the beautiful artwork which so perfectly captures the way looking is a kind of thinking and thinking is a way of looking at the world.

I wrote this book in the three weeks I stayed in Edreen Sheath's inner-city Auckland apartment in April 2024. Thank you so much to Edreen, and to Oli, her magnificent cat, whose wish that I should sit for long hours in the chair by the window kept me working on this laptop project. Thank you to Te Herenga Waka – Victoria University of Wellington, for the research leave, and thank you to the Frank Sargeson Trust for a residency in 2022, during which time many of the thoughts remembered in this book were first thought and recorded.

Thank you to the friends who read this work in manuscript: Nina Mingya Powles, Anne Kennedy, Paula Green, Angelina Sbroma and Helen Rickerby. There is a special shimmering to the work that comes from your reading of it.

Thank you to my family: Mac, Nicki, Cam, Larissa, Max, Genevieve, Juliet, Johnny, Libby, Elvira, Josiah, Simon, and the pets, past and present, in and out of this book. My thoughts are full of you, my life lit up by your presence in the world.